Retire Early with Real Estate

I'm FIRED!: Build Financial Independence with Rental Property

Julian Ashford

ISBN: 9781807650476

Published by TPSA Publishing

Table Of Contents

INTRODUCTION 7

PART 1: GAINING FINANCIAL FREEDOM 9

CHAPTER 1: WHAT IS FINANCIAL FREEDOM? 11

What does this financial freedom mean to you? 11

Learn how to manage your money 12

Clean up your finances 12

Be smart about your career choice 13

Learn about some investment options 14

CHAPTER 2: WHY IS FINANCIAL FREEDOM IMPORTANT TO ME? 17

Freedom from Debt 17

Freedom to Put More Money into Savings 17

Freedom to Do What You Want 18

Freedom to Start Building Your Own Wealth 19

CHAPTER 3: CREATING A BUDGET 21

1. Gather up all the financial statements that you have 21

2. Record all of the income sources that you make 21

3. Create a list of monthly expenses 22

4. Break the expenses up into variable and fixed 22

5. Total out the monthly income and expenses 23

6. Make some adjustments to your expenses 23

CHAPTER 4: CREATING YOUR EMERGENCY FUND 25

1. Set the initial target low 26

2. Creating a retirement plan 27

CHAPTER 5: WORKING ON YOUR CREDIT SCORE 31

Check your credit reports to see if they are accurate 31

Pinpoint out what you need to report 32

Create a plan to improve your credit score 34

CHAPTER 6: PASSIVE INCOME STREAMS TO HELP YOU REACH YOUR GOALS OF FINANCIAL FREEDOM 37

Investing time 37

Investing money 38

Working with real estate to make a passive income 38

Other ideas to use 40

CHAPTER 7: SUSTAINING THE MOTIVATION TOWARDS GAINING YOUR FINANCIAL FREEDOM 45

Get Mad at Your Debt 45

Get Rid of Everything 46

Think About Using an Accountability Partner 46

Blog About Your Progress or Keep a Journal 47

Continually Educate Yourself 47

Work on Developing your New Habits 48

Focus on Every Little Step to Get Out of Debt 48

PART 2: RENTAL PROPERTIES: AN ULTIMATE SOURCE OF PASSIVE INCOME 51

CHAPTER 8: WHY SHOULD I CHOOSE RENTAL PROPERTIES AS MY SOURCE OF PASSIVE INCOME? 53

Why are rental properties so good for passive income? 53

CHAPTER 9: BASIC STEPS TO PURCHASING A RENTAL PROPERTY 57

1. Researching the market 57

2. Considering a real estate agent 57

3. Finding the first property 58

5. Putting in an offer 60

6. Doing the inspections 61

7. Checking out the title 61

8. Closing on the property 62

9. Fixing it up quickly 62

10. Finding the right tenants 63

11. Maintaining the property 63

CHAPTER 10: HOW TO TURN YOUR PROPERTY INTO A PASSIVE INCOME 65

1. Do your research 65

CONCLUSION 69

INTRODUCTION

Congratulations on downloading *Retire Early with Real Estate* and thank you for doing so.

The following chapters will discuss everything that you need to know in order to get started with your own real estate endeavor. All of us think about and dream about our retirement. We look forward to the days when we can stop working and can just sit back and enjoy the things that you have missed while working so hard. But when you take a look at some of the tips in this guidebook and learn how to work with real estate and rental properties, you can reach your financial freedom today, rather than waiting until you are too old to enjoy it

This guidebook is going to spend some time looking at what financial freedom means, how to get your finances in order with a budget and a good emergency fund, and how to increase your credit score. You won't be able to handle any of the investments that you are interested in, especially when it comes to rental properties, without taking out some money along the way, and a good credit score can be key to making this easier. We will then move on to some of the best passive income streams and sources you can work with to reach your goals, and some of the ways that you can make sure that you keep yourself motivated to actually retire early with real estate.

Once we have a good understanding of how this process works and what needs to happen in order to get your finances in order and start reaching for that financial freedom, we will dive right into some of the things that you need to do to get started with rental properties. Rental properties and really all real estate endeavors are some of the best things that you can do in order to make a passive income and earn some serious profits.

In this section, we will take a look at why rental properties are the best source of passive income, some of the steps that you need to take in order to get started with investing in rental properties, and how to turn these rental properties into a passive income once you get it all set up.

Many of us dream about the day when we are going to reach our own financial freedom and be able to quit our jobs and retire. Why not make that day sooner than your original thought? Take some time to look through this guidebook to help you get started with gaining your financial freedom with the help of rental properties.

There are plenty of books on this subject on the market, thanks again for choosing this one! Every effort was made to ensure it is full of as much useful information as possible, please enjoy!

PART 1: GAINING FINANCIAL FREEDOM

CHAPTER 1: WHAT IS FINANCIAL FREEDOM?

We have all gone through the experience. We have a panic that starts to set into our stomach when we see the bill for when the car broke down without notice. We become panicked worrying about how we are going to pay for that repair. But how would it feel if that car repair wasn't as big of a deal, just more of an inconvenience rather than something that put us in a deep sweat? You can pay that bill without all of the worries and a week later you forget that this bill even happened!

Does the latter situation make you feel a sense of relief? This is what financial freedom can do for you. Being able to pay for some of the unexpected things that show up in your life won't be the end of the world. You will be able to pay off that bill without going further into debt or missing out on other important things that you need to deal with.

Financial freedom is more than just being able to go through and afford some of the emergencies that show up in your life. It is more about knowing that you can relieve yourself of paying for retirement because you have set it up with a financial investor. It is the freedom to quit your regular job so that you can actually do something that you enjoy and like, rather than having to work for the paycheck.

Financial freedom means that you will be able to make a lot of your life decisions without feeling too stressed out about the financial impact that it will cause you and your family because you are prepared. You are able to control the finances, rather than letting them control you.

Keep in mind though that this financial freedom isn't going to be a get rich quick strategy. If someone starts to sell you something like that, then you need to run quickly in the other direction. You will have to put in some hard work, you will need to sacrifice some, and it can take a few years or more. But if you take the time to work towards your financial freedom now, you will be able to gain it in time.

What does this financial freedom mean to you?

In order to really reach financial freedom, it needs to be personal. Dream big, and then take some time to get specific about your goal. Think for a moment about what this financial independence looks like for you. Some examples of what you may like for your own personal freedom include:

- Freedom to retire ten or more years early without having to worry about money.
- The freedom to be able to respond to the needs of others with a lot of generosity.

- Freedom to go out and get a new ski boat or car or another larger purchase and pay cash for it.
- The freedom to take a big trip, or even fly internationally, without having a big strain on your budget.
- The freedom to choose a career that you love without having to worry too much about the money.

When you learn how to be financially independent, you are going to have some options. You won't have to wonder about whether the bank account that you have is able to handle the things that come up on a regular basis for your life, such as buying groceries, getting your hours cut at work, or having to take care of the water heater when it needs to be replaced.

While reaching financial freedom may seem like it is too good to be true, it is actually something that you are able to do. There are a few things that you are able to do in order to help you to reach this freedom and we are going to look at them below:

Learn how to manage your money

It is impossible for you to get ahead with your money if you don't have a good plan for your money. Instead, you will get to the end of each month and then wonder where all of the money went? This is more of a financial disaster rather than the financial independence that you are looking for. If you are single, you will be able to do this on your own. But if you are married, you will need to sit down and be on the same page with your spouse.

Building up the wealth is impossible if you are spending your life living paycheck to paycheck. To manage your money, you need to take the time to give every dollar a name before the month gets started. then you need to track the way that you spend for that month. If you find that there are areas that you are consistently underspending or overspending even if you are trying to be careful, then it is time to consider adjusting the amount that you put into each category.

Budgeting, as we will discuss in a bit, will be so important when it comes to helping you get your finances on the right track. But it doesn't need to end here. Once you are to this financial freedom, you will need to keep up with your budget each month. It doesn't matter how much money you have; you must make sure that you have a plan in place for the money, or you will become broke again and have to start over.

Clean up your finances

Once you have taken some time to learn how to manage your money, you may notice that you have made some financial mistakes Don't feel bad; everyone has been in that situation at one point or another. But if you want to make sure that you gain that financial freedom, then you need to clean up the mess that you are in, and then you can build up more of the wealth as you want.

This means that if you have car loans, student loans, or credit cards, it is time for you to start getting serious about handling these and getting them gone. Why do you need to do this? Basically, if you owe any money, your paycheck is going to have someone else's name on them and it is harder for you to reach your goals.

Paying off all of the debts that you have right now is really the foundation for helping you build up wealth that will last. Before you start, set aside $1000. Whether you do this with your regular job or through the passive income streams, like rental properties, that we discuss below, doesn't matter. But having that put away can help if an emergency comes up and won't throw your budget out.

Once that is set up, you are able to go through and start paying down your debts as aggressively as possible. Any extra that you make from your regular job, any side jobs and income, and more should go straight to the debts. It may mean that you have to forgo some of the things that you want to do for a bit. But it can also ensure that you get the debts paid off and will be able to keep more of the money in your own pocket.

Be smart about your career choice

The biggest way that you are able to build up your wealth is your income. So, when you are ready to choose your career, there are a few things that are at stake. There is no reason that you have to stay at a job that isn't going anywhere and that makes you feel miserable of course, but being smart can help you bring in enough money to pay off your debts and start to pay off your debts.

This brings up the question of what you need to look for when you are trying to decide which career you are the most interested in. Some of the things that you can keep in mind and consider when trying to pick a career that will help you reach your goals of building wealth include:

1. What are your goals and where would you like to be in the next decade. You should start out with the end in mind. Does the job you are looking at make sense with the overall goals that you have?
2. Is there some potential for earning more income later on? You may have to start out with a salary that is a bit lower. But make sure that this opportunity does include an income increase in the future as your value increases. If it doesn't, then it is time to look for another career to help you reach your goals.

3. Can you grow? Are there some opportunities present that will help you move up and grow, both in your professional and personal life?
4. Do you like the work? You don't want to spend that much of your time working in a career or a job that you can't stand. Find something that speaks to your passions a bit and will allow you to use your skills and gifts to get ahead.
5. Do the benefits make it easier for you to reach financial freedom? Your options for health insurance and for retirement savings can really make an effect on your ability to build up the wealth that you want.

Learn about some investment options

Once you have been able to take some time to put away a bit of money in your savings, such as the $1000 to ensure that you are able to handle any of the emergencies that come your way, it is time to start learning how to put your money to work for you. This is one of the best ways to ensure that you are able to reach the financial freedom that you are looking for.

You are only able to work so many hours of the day. Even if you and your spouse are both working one or two jobs each, this may cut into the time that you get to spend with each other and your children. And when it comes to the costs of daycare, you may find that you still need money to pay things off and gain financial freedom. But since we can't work 24/7, it is sometimes better to find other options to build up your wealth.

Working with investments can be one of the best options here. You are able to put some of your money into the investment, and then, with some work, of course, you will see it grow. Many times this can help you to grow your money when you are sleeping. You will have to put in some time, some research, and some sweat to make it work, but it can become much more profitable than working with your regular job. And if it is done in the right manner, you will be able to even turn it into a full-time income and really gain financial freedom.

There are a lot of great investment options that you can choose to work with depending on your needs and how much you would like to do with this financial freedom. Some of the options include:

1. Retirement savings

This is one investment that everyone needs to work on as soon as possible. Each year that you are able to put into the retirement account, even if it is a small amount, can make a difference of thousands over the years. Thanks to the deposits that you make, any potential employer matches, and compound interest, you can earn a lot on this investment for your retirement.

Find a good financial advisor and learn how to take advantage of all the retirement accounts that are available to you. Consider how much you should try to invest in your retirement. Anything can be helpful, but going for 15 percent is a good place to start.

There are a few retirement accounts that you can choose from but a Roth IRA is a good idea for a lot of people after you have gotten a company match at work. The Roth IRA means that the money you invest is going to grow tax-free. Once you withdraw that money during your retirement, it is going to not have any taxes due on it and can be a huge benefit when you get to retirement since you are most likely going to lose most of your deductions, such as child tax credit, by that time.

2. Real estate investments

Your home can be a big part of your plan to reach financial freedom, but it also shouldn't be something that holds you back. That's why it is so important to make some good decisions about the home that you are going to purchase, and the way that you choose to finance it. If you stay within your budget, can come up with a good down payment, and pick a home that actually suits your needs, then you will find that it will continue to grow in value throughout the years.

After you have been able to invest 15 percent of your income into a retirement account, you can take this extra money to pay off your home. And as soon as you are able to do that, start attacking the mortgage with a vengeance. Once you are able to get rid of that mortgage and the hundreds (and sometimes way more) that it costs you each month is a huge milestone that can help you to have extra money that you want to use each month for your own needs.

Rental properties can be a great option to invest in at this time. There is some advice that you should wait until you pay off your own home before you invest in rental properties. This can make it easier for you to get a new mortgage on the property without having to make two payments.

3. Taxable investments

You can also work on taxable investments. When you have been able to pay off your home, you are then able to contribute more than 15 percent of your income to investments. But before you jump into some of the taxable investments, make sure that you are taking advantage of all the tax-favored accounts that you can, such as your workplace 401(k)

But once you do that, it is time to move into some of the taxable accounts that you are able to work on as well. You should try to stick with an investment approach that is simple as you learn the ropes and what it takes to be successful. Your financial advisor will be able to help you find a good investment, such as a stock mutual fund that is growing strong and has a long history of performing above average.

When you invest outside of your retirement accounts, remember that you will need to pay some taxes on that money. You should also be ready to pay some taxes on any of the qualified dividends and capital gains that you see. But the best option here is to choose mutual funds with a low turnover rate that will help you to minimize your tax impact.

How to be active in this journey to reach financial independence

Making the right investment decisions is just the first step that you need to follow. But you also have to make sure that you are in tune with the performance of your funds to ensure that you are able to get the most out of these. You also have to be careful and make sure that you are keeping with your budget and really working to keep your finances in line. Otherwise, it won't matter how much you make on your investment, it will all go down the drain.

You will find that working with a financial advisor can be a great option to help you get results. A financial advisor is going to help you in a number of ways including:

1. Helping you to make good decisions about your investment strategy.
2. Can help you to do any balancing of the funds that are necessary so that you can minimize your risks.
3. Can help you create a plan that is realistic to you and can help you see what this financial independence is going to look like for you.
4. Helps you to know which investment options you have beyond just doing a retirement account.
5. Can make sure that a good withdrawal plan is in place based on your specific situation.

Reaching financial freedom is going to be a bit different for everyone involved. You may decide to get a second job, just pay down debts so that you can go after a job you love, or you may choose to invest your money and earn income from stocks, dividends, or rental properties. But figuring out what financial freedom means to you is going to make a big difference and can help you to get the results that you want, without dreading your job or being in debt for years to come.

CHAPTER 2: WHY IS FINANCIAL FREEDOM IMPORTANT TO ME?

Financial freedom can mean a little something different for each person who is trying to achieve it. It is sometimes hard to imagine it because we often fall pretty to all of the advertisements and more that hound us from one day to the next. Many of us are in a lot of debt and don't know how we are ever going to be able to get rid of it. But understanding why financial freedom is so important to us, and taking the steps to make it our priority can make a world of difference in how much success we can have with this goal.

There are actually quite a few benefits of reaching your own financial freedom, and as you start to get closer to achieving that goal, you will start to see how beneficial it can be to your overall goals and helping you to get some of the other things that you want out of life. Some of the best benefits that come with earning your own financial freedom include:

Freedom from Debt

Imagine how it will feel. Imagine how your lie would change when there isn't any more debt! What would you be able to do if you no longer had to put your money towards credit cards, loans, mortgages, or any of the other debts that you have to deal with on a regular basis?

Instead of having to pay in all of this money to creditors for things that you purchased or used in the past, along with the interest that comes with it, you can take all of that extra money, which could be hundreds of dollars a month, into your cash reserves and investments.

While it may seem like in our very consumerist world that this is an impossible dream, if you work on it and are willing to give up some of the instant gratifications that come in our modern world, you will be able to make this a reality. It won't always be easy, but it won't take long for you to notice the good benefits that come with this endeavor.

Freedom to Put More Money into Savings

When you aren't putting as much into your debts and paying off the creditors you have, you will find that it is easier to put more money into your savings. Many times it is hard to save. We either assume that we have no extra money to put into savings because we spend so much on little things that we don't need. Or we start to accumulate savings and then we see all of that extra money that is in the account, and we want to go and spend it on something big.

Your savings can be so important to your overall goal of financial freedom. While you don't have to add money to your savings and never touch all of it again, it is good to keep at least a little bit of money in your savings to help you out when things go wrong. While we always hope and pray that the worst will never happen, things aren't always in our control. Having some savings for an emergency fund can make all of the difference in helping you to stay secure and not have to worry about your finances all of the time.

Some people wonder why they should put money into a savings account if you aren't able to get very much interest from it. Since most savings accounts have such a low-interest rate on them, wouldn't it be better to invest the money instead? Savings is something that we naturally do when we start to spend less money than we have. If your income is exceeding your spending, you are going to have some cash around that you are able to use as you wish. You can save to build up a nice cash reserve, or to use to help you if a good investment opportunity comes your way.

Basically, it is always a good idea to have some sort of savings. You can use it or a good investment opportunity that comes your way. you can use it to help when emergencies happen. It is always a good idea to keep a bit of extra money to the side, whether it is in cash or in a savings account, for when the opportunity arises, this is true financial freedom.

Freedom to Do What You Want

Think about how nice it will be in order to go out and do what you want/ While financial freedom doesn't mean that you can go and be crazy with your money and spend it without budgeting and being careful. But it does mean that you could consider new investment options, going on vacation more often, and having more of the fun and freedom that you are looking for.

When you aren't going to have to pay your income to the creditors all of the time, you are able to do a lot. you can take that money and travel. You can use it to move to a new place, you can start your own business. You can make some big decisions without having to spend all of your time and energy focusing on how much it is going to cost or if you have the money that it requires.

Freedom From All of the Stress that Comes from Your Finances

There is nothing that causes as much stress on you, both as an individual and as a couple, then your finances. Having to worry about the cost of things, whether you are going to have enough money to pay for the things that you and your family need, And when you and your spouse are both working hard in order to get things paid off, and there still doesn't seem to be enough to get through the month, it can be even more frustrating.

Stress about finances can be the worst. You may feel like you are stuck and won't be able to get out of the debt without a miracle. It can cause a lot of fights between spouses because they are tired and worn out, and they are trying to find a way to make it better.

But think about how it would feel if you were able to avoid all of these problems and hassles? What if you weren't having to fight with your spouse each month in order to pay the bills and make things work out because you knew that you actually had enough in the account and saved up to handle it? What if you didn't have to worry so much, and you were actually able to do some of the things that you want, without having to sacrifice food and other things that you need each month.

Freedom to Start Building Your Own Wealth

When you work to reach the financial freedom that you need, you will find that wealth will be created. But you will only be able to create this wealth if you are able to create positive cash flow. If more money is going out each month than you are making, or if you are breaking even, then how are you ever going to be able to build up wealth?

The nice thing with financial freedom is that you are able to step in and be able to put money into savings and use it the way that you would like. And the more that you are able to pay back, thanks to a higher income or less debt, the easier it is for you to build up the wealth that you want.

There are so many reasons why you would want to choose to gain your own financial freedom. No one likes to be in debt all of the time. They aren't interested in sending a ton of their hard earned money to the creditors in order to pay off debts for things that they no longer use or appreciate. We all want to be able to go on vacations, take days off when we want, and even retire early without having to worry all of the time. And this is where financial freedom and the steps that are listed in this guidebook will help you to reach these goals and see the results and the benefits that you want.

CHAPTER 3: CREATING A BUDGET

If you are trying to work on gaining your financial freedom, and you want to be able to start a second income, your own business, and even in real estate, then you need to make sure that you are in full control over your money. Many Americans run into issues with controlling their money, and they end up with more month than money. This is not the best way to ensure that you are able to control your financial future.

Coming up with a budget is one of the best things that you can do in order to gain the control that you need for your money. This budget can be as detailed as you want. You can plan down to every last little thing that you are going to spend your money on, or you can generalize a bit and have categories of money that you are going to spend on.

Before you take the time to start on your budget, it is important to realize that to make it successful; you need to provide as much detailed and accurate information on it as possible. The hope with this is that the end result of this budget is going to give you a full picture of where your money comes from, how much there is, and where you are sending it each month. Once this is figured out, you are able to make the changes that you need to the budget so that you have more control over what is coming in, and what is going out each month.

Here, we are going to take some time to look at the steps that you need to follow in order to create your own budget. There are a few steps that you can take in order to create a budget and actually get the financial freedom that you desire.

1. Gather up all the financial statements that you have

The more information that you have, the easier it is to start this kind of budget. You should gather all of the financial documents and statements that you can including recent utility bills, investment accounts, bank statements, and anything else that will give you information about the source of expense or income that you have.

One thing that you are going to find as key when you are working on this budget is that you need to create a monthly average. This helps you to find the average that you tend to spend from one month to another, and the average that you make, even if there is variation in the equation. The more information that you are able to dig up about this, the easier it is to come up with that monthly average.

2. Record all of the income sources that you make

Right now, you may just have your own job and the job of a spouse. This can make it easier to do this step. But if you have any side income that you rely on each month, then this needs to be calculated into the budget as well.

If you work on the side, are a freelancer, are self-employed, earn money from any of your investments, or make any other outside sources of income, then you need to take the time to record these as well. If you have your income reach you in the form of a regular paycheck from your employer and the taxes are taken out of that for you, then using the net income or the take-home pay, the amount is going to be fine for this.

Bring out some paper and write down all of the sources of income that you have, or that you and your spouse have. You can then write this amount down as the income for the month that you are going to use on the rest of this budget plan we are going to make.

3. Create a list of monthly expenses

The next thing to work on is to write down a list of all the expenses that you plan to pay or deal with over the next month. You will want to include the regulars like retirement savings, student loans, dry cleaning if you use it, entertainment, utilities, groceries, insurance, car payments, and mortgage payments. If you have anything else you have to spend during the month, such as credit card payments, then these need to be set up as well.

You should also consider setting aside a little bit in savings. This can be useful for when emergencies come up that you weren't expecting, or if you would like to be able to save up for something that is a bigger purchase. It is always best to have a little bit of money saved up to help you out when these emergencies happen.

Make sure that you are honest with yourself here. You want to be able to have a good clear picture of the things that you are spending your money on here. Only you and your spouse, if you are doing it with them, will see this money, so you don't have to hide it from anyone else. But looking at your bank and credit card statements and making sure that all of the expenses are listed out can give you a full picture of your finances.

After you have this information down, you will be able to go through and think about the things that everyone can cut out. If you aren't home enough to watch television, maybe cut out the $100 cable bill each month. If you see that you are eating out a few times a week, maybe cut one or two of those out each month to save money. Each family is different in the way that they spend their money. But having a complete list of monthly expenses can give you a good idea of what you need to cut back on to see the best results for your family.

4. Break the expenses up into variable and fixed

To start, we need to look at the fixed expenses. These are going to be the ones that stay about the same from one month to the next, and they are the ones that you need to pay from one month to another to maintain your way of living. This would include things like your trash pickup, your cable or internet service, car payments, or your mortgage and rent. These expenses are usually not going to change from one month to another, though you can throw a bit extra money at them each month if you wish to get them paid off faster.

Then there are the variable expenses. These are the ones that will change from one month to the next. They can include gifts for friends and family, eating out, entertainment, gasoline, and groceries. This is the one that you will need to pay attention to when you try to make some adjustments to your spending and try to reign in your budget a little bit.

5. Total out the monthly income and expenses

If you are going through all of this and you notice that the end result shows that you have more income than expenses, then this means that you are off to a good start. You will be able to prioritize this excess to the areas of your budget, such as paying off your credit card or putting more into your retirement savings.

If you are like most people though, you will find that the income and debt come pretty close, or the expenses are higher than your income. In both of these cases, if you want to gain the financial freedom that you are promised, then you will need to go through and make some adjustments to either your income, your expenses, or to both.

6. Make some adjustments to your expenses

If you have taken the time to accurately list out all of the expenses that you are dealing with each month, then the ultimate goal for you is to have the income and the expenses come in as equal. This allows you to account for your income - either it was budgeted for your expenses or for savings.

But if you are looking at the budget and you notice that the expenses end up higher than the income that you make each month, then it is time to look through the variable expenses and see if there are some areas that you are able to cut. Since these as the expenses that are considered non-essential, or will have some wiggle room when it comes to how much you can spend, you should be able to cut out a few dollars from them if you tighten your belt in order to make this easier.

If you are already cutting down on a lot of things, and have given up on those things that you no longer need, such as the cable and internet to save some money or cut out how many times you go out to eat during the week, but your expenses still are too high, it may be time to bring in another income. This will help you to make sure that you are bringing in enough money to cover your debts. And even if you do make enough to cover your debts each month, you may still want to bring in a second income to help build up your financial freedom.

Another thing to consider is that you need to go through and review your budget on a regular basis. This ensures that you are going to always stay on track. After you get through the first month, sit down and compare the actual expenses versus what you had placed in the budget. And then do this every few months after that. This is going to show you where you did well, and where you need to improve to make the budget work.

CHAPTER 4: CREATING YOUR EMERGENCY FUND

When you are working to reach your financial freedom, you want to make sure that you take the time to create a nice emergency fund. You don't want to put in all of this work and find out that all of it is ruined because a medical bill, something on the car needs to be fixed, or some other unexpected expense comes up during the month.

But before we work on making this fund, we need to understand what the emergency fund is. an emergency fund is going to be any of the cash that you have been able to save up and the only purpose of it is helping you to maintain your normal life through any emergencies that come your way. For the most part, you will not touch this emergency fund. It is going to sit in the account, hopefully making some interest and waiting until a time when you can actually use it. When you lose your job when an appliance breaks down or something else comes up.

Many of the people who don't already have this fund will see the idea of having it as a type of punishment. After all, they see this money being locked up in a savings account and since they can't use it, they can't have it to help them live or have any fun. And this can seem like a depressing thought.

But once you create this fund, you will see that it is actually the opposite – that having this fund actually means that you have a bit of room to breathe. You won't be in a complete panic if the car breaks down or you need to replace the hot water heater and weren't expecting it. Instead of having to stress out and try to find a way to squeeze those expenses onto a credit card, take out another loan, or ask someone for the money, you can use your emergency fund, and not have to worry about it.

You do have to be careful to not spend the money on things that aren't actually seen as emergencies. This can be a big temptation and can take you away from actually getting the things covered that are emergencies. It is easy to see that you have built up a few hundred dollars or more in savings and then they will choose to use it for other things that aren't emergencies, such as going on a trip or getting a new television, just because they wanted to.

If you want to start up a second savings account, one that is for those big splurges, then that is fine. Go ahead and work on a splurge fund if that is what makes the most sense for you. But make sure that this is separate from the emergency fund. In fact, set up your emergency fund, deposit money into it each month, and then never look again at the balance until you actually come across an emergency.

Now that we know a bit about the emergency fund, it is time to explore the first steps that you need to take to start up your emergency fund. These will include the following:

1. Set the initial target low

It may seem tempting for you to go through and try to bite off a huge goal for that emergency fund right from the start. But when the goal is big, you may find that it is hard to get there, and you lose all of your motivation. And then when you do have a few emergencies to take care of with that money, and the fund gets depleted a bit, you may become even more discouraged in the process.

Deciding to go for eight months of living expenses can be a big goal for a lot of people, and it could take a few years or more to get there depending on what your budget is and how much you make. And going with this large of a goal is bound to make you feel disheartened along the way.

Instead of starting out with a goal that is this big, it is better to go with one that is a bit more reasonable. You maybe can start by having an emergency fund goal that is $250 or $500. You can probably get to that in a few months, or even less if you have a really great income situation. But this is often the amount that is big enough that it can help you out when you do run into the emergency situation where the money is needed.

Then, you can break up that big goal into smaller pieces. Perhaps you are able to put away $25 a week at this time. this means that after ten weeks, you would reach your goal of having $250 in your emergency fund. Maybe you are able to get $40 a week away for this, which means that you will get to the goal of $500 in just three months.

You want to start with a goal that you are able to actually reach, and in a shorter amount of time. This can encourage you to keep working hard to get that goal again. From there, you can really start to see it grow even more. But you have to start somewhere.

The issue that a lot of people run into here though is wondering how they are going to come up with the extra money each week. It may not sound like a lot, but when you are first getting started, your budget may be low and you are uncertain about where you will be able to call up that extra money.

The good news is that there are actually a lot of ways that you will be able to move around your budget and add in some more breathing room in order to get that emergency room funded. Some of the options that you can choose to free up even a few dollars in your budget each month include:

- First, see if you are able to get a rate reduction on the credit cards. If you are working with a balance on your credit card, getting the interest rate reduced is going to help you save a lot of money each month. The way to do this is to turn the card over, call the number that is on the back, and ask to speak with a supervisor. Then from there, you can ask if they are willing to reduce your rate. You may find that discussing transferring the balance of the card over to one with a lower interest rate. If they are not willing to reduce the balance of the card, you may want to consider going with a card that has no interest in transfers, which can help you to pay it off faster.

- You can also consider looking around for better homeowners and auto insurance. There are often different rates for the various services that you use. You can shop around a bit to figure out if you are able to get the coverage that you want for a lower price.
- Before you go shopping, make sure that you use a shopping list. If you take at least ten minutes of planning before you go to the store can save you a lot of time at the store. Plus, it ensures that you are able to get everything that you need when you are at the store without leaving anything behind and having to go back and forth. Plus, it ensures that you don't put anything that is unnecessary into the cart that you don't need and that costs too much money.
- Next on the list is to change out one splurge a month. Instead of going out to eat for a more expensive dinner each month, turn that into a meal that you eat at home, or go somewhere that doesn't cost as much. Even if you choose to prepare something that is a bit fancier in your own home, it is still going to save you a lot of money in the process.
- See if you can change around the way that you get from one location to another. You may find someone who lives close to you and take turns carpooling to get where you want to be. If you can, consider using a bike or public transportation rather than using a vehicle. This can save you on gas money, and may even make it so that you can reduce yourself to one car and save on the costs of fixing it up and the issues with gas, insurance, and more.
- And of course, if you can look over your budget and see a few other ways that you can trim things don, then you definitely need to do this as well. Do you find that you don't really have time to sit and watch television? Then cut out the cable. Do you find that you don't use that subscription service that you are signed up for? Then cut it. Every little thing that you are able to cut out of your budget can save you a lot of money and makes it easier for you to save your emergency fund.

2. Creating a retirement plan

While we are on the topic of creating savings and why it is so important, we need to take a few minutes to also explore the importance of starting your retirement plan. No matter what age you are right now or the age that you plan to retire, setting up a good retirement plan can make a world of difference. This is the ultimate show of your financial freedom. If you are able to put enough away in savings, and into your retirement plan, to retire on time, and even early, then you are free to quit your job and actually enjoy the life that you have!

Starting your retirement savings as early as possible is one of the best choices. It is never too late to start this retirement account, but it is also never too early either. Each year that you are able to put at least something into the retirement, even if you are not able to max out the account, could result in thousands of extra dollars to use in retirement. And for how much you are putting in, thanks to compound interest, you will earn a ton in its place.

There are a few different options of retirement plans that you can choose to work with. The one that is the best for you will depend on your own unique situation. First off is the 401 (k). If you have an employer who is offering to match some of your contributions, then you definitely need to choose this one. At least put in enough to get the full match from your employer. This is free money that you can put away from retirement, and it will earn the compound interest just the same as the money you add in. take advantage of this to help bolster up your own retirement plan.

If you are looking to get a tax break because of some of your other investments, then this retirement plan can help as well. The money that you place into these accounts will not be taxed for that year. So, if you make $60,000 and put $6000 into one of these retirement accounts, you will only be taxed $54,000 for that year. This can help you to lower your tax bill and help you budget a bit better.

There is a drawback to using this though. Since you are not being taxed on this income right when you earn it, you will be taxed when you withdraw the money. All of the money that you put into the account, along with any of the money you earned from the investments and compound interest, are going to be taxable. Since you are less likely to have deductions like children, home, and student loan interest rates, this can end up being a larger tax bill when you retire.

Another option is to work with a Roth IRA. These work in a similar manner to the other option above, but the taxes are a bit different. With these, if you earn $60,000 for the year and put $6000 away, you will still be taxed on the $60,000. But when you withdraw the money during retirement, all of the money that you put in, plus the money that the investments made will be tax-free!

Since many of us have more tax deductions when we are younger, such as our children and our homes, compared to what we will have when we retire, this is often the choice to make. You can then withdraw as much of the money as you want during retirement, without having to worry about the tax bill at the end of the year. Of course, you should be modest, but it can make it easier to budget when you reach retirement.

The next thing to look at is how much you should put into your retirement. Most people agree that between 10 to 15 percent of your income is ideal to help you get a nice nest egg saved up for those years. But if you are dealing with debts and trying to get your finances in order, don't let that number scare you. Anything is better than nothing. Don't let it keep you away from investing in your retirement right now because any little bit can help and will add up over time.

Even if you are only able to put a few hundred dollars, or even less, away a month to your retirement, that is something. Your financial advisor will be able to invest that money for you and ensures that you can earn something. And as the years go on and compound interest comes into play, and you add more money in each month, you will see what a difference even that small amount will be able to make to the final number you have in your account at retirement.

It is so important for you to take some time for you to learn how to save. Whether it is an emergency fund, money for retirement, or money for some of those big purchases that you need to focus on, it is so important for you to make savings a priority. Doing even a little bit now may not seem like much, but it will make a big difference in the amount of financial freedom that you can enjoy.

CHAPTER 5: WORKING ON YOUR CREDIT SCORE

As you are working towards improving your financial situation and gaining more financial freedom, there are likely to be times when you will need to borrow money to make this happen. When we talk about starting in rental properties later in this guidebook, it is unlikely that you will have $100,000 or more sitting around in order to purchase the property. Instead, you will need to take out a mortgage or another loan to help you do this. But before any lending institute will provide you with that money, you need to have a good credit score.

It is important that you start working on your credit score right now. All of us have troubles at some time with our credit score, but you need to make sure that you get it fixed as soon as possible. These credit scores aren't going to improve for you overnight, so working on it as soon as possible can make a big difference.

There are a few different things that you are able to do in order to help improve your credit score, and a lot of it can be done starting now. These include:

Check your credit reports to see if they are accurate

The first thing that you need to do to check out your credit score is to look at the credit reports. Everyone is going to have tree credit reports, and these come from the three major credit bureaus: TransUnion, Equifax, and Experian. These credit reports will often have some mistakes on them, but it is your job to go through and double check to see if these mistakes are there.

According to a study from the Federal Trade Commission, it was found that one in five consumers had an error on one or more of their credit reports. And then the study that was done in 2015 to follow up found that those who reported this unresolved error on their credit reports still believed that one piece of disputed information is still inaccurate on the report.

Since the credit score that you have is going to be based on these credit reports, it is so important to make sure that the information that is on these reports is as accurate as possible. If you find that there is a discrepancy or a mistake on the report, then the credit score is going to show that mistake until you make some changes.

It is easy to go through and check the credit report from each of these reporting agencies. You are able to get a free copy each year from all three agencies thanks to the Fair Credit Reporting Act. Most credit scores, including the FICO score, will operate within the range of 300 and 85-. The tiers of the various credit scores are going to reflect the following:

1. **Excellent scores 750+**

2. **Good credit = 700-749**
3. **Fair credit = 650-699**
4. **Poor credit 600-649**
5. **Bad credit is below 600**

Once you have these three reports for credit in hand, there are a few questions that you should take the time to ask yourself to make sure that you are able to find the errors that you need. These include:

1. Is all of the personal information on the report accurate? Is your name, address, birth date, social security number and all the other personal information that is on the report accurate?
2. Are all of the accounts that you have credit with reported on these?
3. Are there any missed or late payments on the report that you know you made on time?
4. Are there any applications for credit, or any accounts, that you don't remember?
5. Are there any items that are decades old and shouldn't be there that are still showing up on the report.

It is going to help you to go through the credit report with your highlighter and then pick out any and all of the inconsistencies that are there. remember that the credit report from one of the reporting agencies may have an error, but then one of the others doesn't have this error. This is why you need to check all of your reports, rather than just going with one of the reports and calling that good enough.

In addition, if you find that there is the same error on all of your credit reports, then you have to take some time to dispute this separately with each of the credit bureaus since each of them are their own entities. And then if there is more than one error on the report, you have to go through and file a separate dispute for each of the errors that you have.

Pinpoint out what you need to report

Now that you have your credit reports in hand and you have checked out any of the errors and made sure to get them fixed as much as possible, it is time to look at the report and decide what you should improve. Simply because you have an error on the report doesn't mean that this is the reason you have bad credit. A misspelled name doesn't mean that your credit is bad because of this. But there are some other things that can happen on your report, ones that aren't errors, and you need to figure out what these are and work on fixing them.

If it is because of an error on your credit report, then there are a few different reasons why the errors are there, and you need to figure out which one it is in order to make the changes that are necessary. These include:

1. Your identity is stolen and there is someone else who is abusing your credit. You will need to go through and deal with this problem to help get your score back on track.
2. A collection account that is really old is still being reported, even when it goes past the statute of limitation in your state. You can report this error and usually get it removed.
3. A bill that your ex is responsible for paying, according to your divorce, have gone unpaid for a while and you are the one who has to deal
4. You defaulted on one of your loans, but now it is showing up as more than one default because it has been sold on to more than one debt collector.
5. Your credit information has been mixed with that of someone else who has a similar name or similar social security number.

If you are taking a look through your credit report and you see that it is accurate, but there are still issues because you have a bad credit score, then it is time to understand why this score is so bad. Some of the factors and how each one is able to impact your credit score.

1. Payment history: If you have any kind of history of making payments late to your creditors, you are going to look like a bigger risk in the future. This one is going to have a bigger effect on your credit score. Start making payments on time and never miss one if you want to fix this.
2. The amount of debt you have. Debt is going to contribute about 30 percent to your FICO score calculation and it is easier to clean up compared to the payment history. This is because if you have five maxed out credit cards, the creditors are going to worry about whether you are able to take out more credit and if you will be able to pay them back. Lower your debt a little bit, and you will be able to increase your score.
3. Age of accounts: If you are newer to the world of borrowing and credit, then there isn't a ton of data there to make your credit score. You may need to just let more time go on your report to help increase the score.
4. Account ix: Lenders want to make sure that you are able to handle different credit types like auto loans and credit cards. So,

if you just have credit cards on the account, it could cause a lowering of the score.

5. History of credit applications: If you went out and applied for a lot of credit this month, the creditor is going to wonder why. They may be worried that you are trying to overextend yourself financially.

Create a plan to improve your credit score

If you look at the credit report and notice that all of the information is accurate, and you know what to do to improve it, you need to make an action plan. You can work with a Credit.com account to see where your credit is and then how your plan, and different actions, will impact the credit score before you start. There are even tips that you can follow on this site and more to help you to get started with improving your score.

There are a number of things that you are able to do in order to help improve your credit score, and working on all of them will make a big difference to that score and what you are able to do in the future. Some of the things that you should consider include:

- Keep credit card balances to a minimum make sure that you keep all of your balances on the credit cards to a minimum. You don't want to take out five cards and then use them all up to the maximum. Make sure to just use them when you need, or to pay bills and then pay right back off when you are done and you will be able to get them to improve your score without making it look bad that you went through and maxed out all of the cards.
- Fix your late payments: Any time that you have a late payment, your credit score is going to be hit hard. It is important that you limit the number of late payments on your score. In fact, start right now in order to never get another late payment. This will help to increase the credit score.
- Clear up the collection accounts: IF there are some collection accounts on your credit report, it is time to go through and try to work on them. If you are able to pay them off, talk to the creditor and see what it takes to get it taken care of and taken off your credit report. Make sure to get it in writing that this will be removed from your report. If the collection agencies are old, make sure to get them removed.
- Limit your credit applications: The more times that you apply for credit, the more it is going to cause harm to your score. Make sure that you only apply for credit when it is needed and be careful about applying for credit too many times near each other.

- Keep the utilization of credit to a minimum: If you have $10,000 limit on your credit cards, make sure that you don't spend $10,000 and keep it at that point too long. If you use it a bit in order to pay some debts and built up your history then that is fine. But you don't want to let the amount get too high. This is going to be one of the factors of your credit score and will impact the results that you are able to get in the process.

Working on your credit score can seem like a big task. It sometimes seems like every little thing can end up causing some big problems with your score. But if you are able to keep these tips and tricks in mind, you will be able to keep your credit score in good working order.

CHAPTER 6: PASSIVE INCOME STREAMS TO HELP YOU REACH YOUR GOALS OF FINANCIAL FREEDOM

One way that you can make sure that you are able to earn your financial freedom is to come up with a way to make a passive income. We only have so many hours in the day and in the week. You may already have a full-time job and are willing to go through and work on a part-time job as well. But these two are going to take up a lot of your time. If you want to spend more time with your family, or you need to make more money, you may be running out of time in the week to do this.

Working with a passive income is a great option to fix this. You have to invest some sort of time or money in order to get started with the passive income, but it is often less than you need to do with some other forms of income, like working for your boss, and you can often fit them in between the other work that you are doing and around your hours.

With a passive income, you will do the work and then can keep making money on the process or the stream without having to keep doing the same amount of work throughout. Writing an eBook and earning the money from it over the years, working with rental properties and collecting the rent on it from your tenants while someone else runs them, and investing in dividend stocks can be seen as options when it comes to taking on a passive income. Let's take a look at some of the other options that you can work with when it is time to bring out a passive income in your life and some of the ones that may work the best for your financial freedom.

Investing time

Most of the time investments that you will work with are going to come together with an investment of energy and ideas as well. For the most part, these investments are going to take some of your spare time and make it provide you with a steady stream of income over time. there are a number of options that you can use when it comes to this form of passive income and that includes:

1. Write a book. EBooks are especially popular right now and can be shown on a wide variety of platforms to reach your guests the best. While you may not be able to make a ton of money, writing a good book with some marketing can help you to earn a little bit of money on the side each month, without having to do more work.
2. Static websites: Another option to work with is to develop a static website that will provide the public with information on a topic they want to know. Then, you can add in some sort of mechanism

to help you make money with it. Affiliate links back to Amazon can be one option.

Investing money

When it comes to most of the investments that you are going to work with to make a passive income stream, you will need to invest at least a little bit of money to make it work. The amount that you will need to spend will depend on how much risk you want to take and what kind of investment you would like to work with. Some of the options to help you earn a passive income through investing your own money include:

1. Dividend-bearing stocks: This is where you will purchase a certain stock then, at predetermined times of the year, the company will pay you a part of their profits, determined on how many stocks you own. If you can find a stock that pays a good amount of dividend each quarter, this can be a lucrative option.

2. Treasury inflation-protected securities: These TIPS are going to be bonds that you are able to purchase from the government. The return on this is going to be low, but the face value will be adjusted according to the interest rates, which means that when it matures, you will be able to sell it for more than you purchased it. These are going to only give you a low rate of return, but they are rock solid investments that will at least match inflation growth when you sell them.

3. CDs and savings accounts. this is a pretty steady investment, but remember that you are not going to make all that much. At most, savings accounts will only make about 2 percent, and that is high, and a CD may only make a slight amount more.

4. Annuities: These are investments that you are able to purchase from your insurance company which is going to pay you a certain amount for the rest of your life. The younger you are when you take it out, the smaller the amount will be.

    a. Let's say that you decide to purchase an annuity that is for $10,000, and the insurance company quotes you for 4 percent. This means that you would be able to receive $400 each year from that annuity for the rest of your life. The risk to this is that the insurance company could become solvent, which means that you would get nothing. Make sure that you pick out a good company to ensure that they are stable and doing well so that you can actually guarantee that you will make money in the process.

Working with real estate to make a passive income

Another thing that you can consider working with is rental properties and real estate to help you make a good passive income. These do take some effort and some investment of money in the beginning, but if you are willing to take some time to learn about the market and to explore all that it has to offer, you will find that it is possible to earn a good income from them, without having to do a lot of work.

Rental properties are usually the best options to go with when it comes to trying to turn your real estate into a passive income. You may need to do all of the work, finding the property, the tenants, and anyone else who needs to help you get this off the ground and running and maintaining the building for the first property or two. But over time, you will be able to leave this work to someone else, such as a property manager, and get to keep the profit while they do all of the work!

There are many individuals and couples who are looking for a place to rent. Maybe they move around often and don't want to get their own place. Maybe they can't get a mortgage for some reason, even though they are able to make all of the payments. They may not want to deal with the costs that are associated with owning your own home. Or they are in college and won't go and get their own property.

As a landlord who is trying to make a passive income from rental properties, you will take some time to find good properties that are offered at lower rates, fix them up, and then rent them out at market prices to ensure that these people have a place to live. If you go through and do it right, you will be able to take the rent payment and use it to pay the mortgage, while pocketing a bit of the amount as well.

Many times the first property is not going to be enough to turn it all into a passive income. While it would be nice to say this is true, you will be lucky to get a single family home to make you a few hundred dollars a month. If you have a multi-unit property, then you may be able to make a little bit more on these properties. Since more than one person is paying into you for the rent. But the amount isn't going to help you to quit your job in the first few months.

The interesting thing is that as you hold onto that first property and build up equity, and you save back even a little of the profits that you make each month, you will be in a great position to turn around and turn this into a way to purchase the second rental property, and then the third rental property and on until you can build up a rental property empire.

With the first handful of buildings, you may be able to do most of the work on your own. This is especially true if you are able to just work with single-family properties. There are only a few tenants you have to deal with at this time and you may find that it is easy enough to handle it on your own to save a bit of money and keep more of your profits in your own pocket.

Over time, as you gain more traction with the real estate empire and get a number of properties under your belt, you can turn this into your own passive income. You will be able to hire a good property manager in order to help you to run the properties. They will collect a bit of the rental money that you receive for doing the work, but if you hire the right company, you will be able to sit back and do other things that you want, or at least take in the second income, without doing all of the work that it takes to maintain and take care of the properties and the tenants.

As you can see, there are a few different options when it comes to working with your own passive income. A passive income can be a great option for you to work with because it ensures that you are able to earn the money, without having to work a regular nine to five job, or having to put in long hours for the long term. With an eBook, you may have to put some time in writing the book and marketing it in the beginning, but you can earn the income for months and years afterward. Rental properties may take some time for you to set up and some hard work in the beginning, but then you can work with a property manager and the money just comes in each month for you.

There are a lot of different passive income sources that you can work with, but one of the best is working with rental properties. There are many people who were able to use the idea of rental properties to help them make a passive income, and it isn't as hard as it may seem!

Other ideas to use

We have spent some time talking about the different things that you can do to earn an income on the side, without having to be present all of the time like you do with your regular 9 to 5 job. This can really help you to grow your wealth, even when you sleep and will help you to gain the financial freedom that you are looking for in no time. Some of the other options that you can choose to work with include:

1. **Buy a business and have someone else run it.** This one may take a bit more investment to get it started, but it can make you a good income in the process. If you can find a franchise or another business where the business owner wants out for retirement or some other reason, you can choose to purchase this. Then, hopefully, the business as good managers and other staff who know what they are doing and are willing to take care of the day to day functioning of that business. You can earn the profits as the new owner of the business, but other people will step in and do all the work of the business for you.

2. **Rent out your car.** This one can be hard if you have a nice car because you need to trust someone else, someone you may not even know, to take good care of your car. You will also need to check out your insurance and make sure that you are covered if someone else does get into an accident or causes other damage to your vehicle. But if you are all set with this one, you will be able to rent out your vehicle to someone else, and take a profit while you aren't using it.
3. **Rideshare.** Uber and Lyft are becoming popular ways for people in big cities to get back and forth to different locations rather than using a taxi. If you have a nice car, can be available during busy times, and you have good insurance that allows for it, then working with the ridesharing idea can be a good option for you.
4. **Use your car to advertise for companies.** Some companies are more than happy to use your car to advertise for them. They are able to put a wrap on the vehicle with their company information. And then you just drive around doing your chores, going to work, going to the grocery store and more, with that decal on. This helps them to drum up some extra business and helps you to earn some new income.
5. **Do cash back on your credit cards.** This one can be a bit tricky. If you got into a lot of debt with credit cards and this is what you are aiming to work on to reach your financial freedom, then do not use this option. But if you are responsible with your money and can use these credit cards wisely, then it could be a great way to earn some money on the side. With these, you would use the credit card for regular purchases and for your bills, and then pay them off right away. You can then earn cash back to use to pay off groceries, vacations, and other things, and it didn't cost you anything extra since you paid off the amount on time and didn't owe in interest.
6. **Take online tasks that are available.** Online tasks are quickly becoming more prevalent as well. Whether it is for writing, doing surveys, watching videos, being virtual assistants, looking things up for others, and more, there are countless tasks that you can now go online and make money in the process.
7. **Sleep studies or other medical studies.** Many medical studies, including sleep studies, are available out there. For a few days of your time, and sometimes some overnight stays, you are able to earn an income, plus help out doctors and scientists throughout the world!

8. **Offer an online guide or course.** Do you have a unique talent that you would like to be able to share with others, one that you can teach? Or do you know some knowledge that others would like to learn about? Then consider coming up with an online guide or doing online courses. You just need to do a few audios or presentations and provide source material, and then the students will do the work after paying for access to that information.

9. **Either start your own blog or purchase a blog.** If you like to blog and have a passion for writing, then you should create your own blog. Come up with a topic that is unique and that you love to write about, and then get started! After you gain some followers, you will be able to do some affiliate links and make money off the products you promote. If you want to invest more now and not take the time, consider purchasing a blog that is already popular, and then monetizing that one.

10. **Rent out the space that you have.** If you have a storage shed, an empty garage, or an extra bedroom or two in your home, why not consider renting it out? You may not be comfortable doing this all of the time, but opening up your home on big holidays or on special weekends can help to bring in a little extra money on space you aren't using.

11. **Investing in the stock market.** There are always a lot of choices when it comes to the stock market. You can work with stocks, bonds, CD's, options, commodities, cryptocurrencies and more. Take some time to explore and see if you are able to find some options that work for you.

12. **Using your own savings account.** This isn't going to provide you a huge return, but if you are already putting some money aside, or if you want to keep some aside in case a good opportunity shows up, then it is worth your time. Before you pick out a savings account, take the time to look at interest rates. Many traditional banks give you less than one percent a year on your money, but there are some online banks that can offer as high as two percent. It isn't a ton, but it can help you to build up your income as the money sits there waiting to be used.

13. **Lending club.** There are some sites out there that will allow you to lend out your money to other people who need it. These are often those who need to pay off their debts or those who want to start a new business. You can set the terms that you are happy with, and then the person you loan it to will accept these terms and pay back the money, along with interest, over time. You often need to have a substantial amount of money to start with this and to make a profit, and you have to really vet each applicant to make sure that they are going to have the resources to pay you the money back.

As you can see, there are a lot of different ways that you are able to make a passive income. Some of them are easier than others, some are going to require more of an initial investment than others, and some you may have no interest in at all. The best way to gain the financial freedom that you are looking for though is to check out a few of them, and consider creating multiple streams of passive income right now!

CHAPTER 7: SUSTAINING THE MOTIVATION TOWARDS GAINING YOUR FINANCIAL FREEDOM

When you first make the decision to get out of debt, it is sometimes easy to feel a lot of excitement about the idea of throwing away the creditor mailings and actually be free of the debt. But getting that job done is actually going to be a much harder thing than you may think in the beginning.

So, the thing to work on here is getting past the potential that you are seeing in yourself and let reality smack you in the face. This may seem tough and a bit rough, but it is going to ensure that you will actually pay attention to what is going on with your debt and gives you a clear picture of what is going on in your life in terms of your debt, and this can help you to get serious about taking care of the debt.

Once you have made the decision to really work on your debt and get rid of it right away, the next thing that you need to take into consideration is that this is going to take some time. while it would be nice to be able to be done with your debts in a few months, or even in a year, it is likely that it can take much longer to get it all paid off. Realizing this right from the start, and understanding that it could take at least a few years to reach the financial freedom that you want can help you to be in the right frame of mind to succeed.

Now that you know all of the benefits of becoming financially free, and you know more about setting up a budget and creating a good emergency fund, it is time to learn some of the steps that you can take in order to motivate yourself to keep going until you get rid of your debts, set up a savings account, and reach your financial freedom.

Get Mad at Your Debt

The best way to help you get started on your debt plan and actually see the results that you want as quickly as possible is to take some time right now getting mad at your debt. Adding emotion to the debt, like anger, is going to help you to really work on eliminating it better than before.

How do you get angry at your debt? Think about how much it is holding you back in your life. When you have to send in that $400 student loan payment, think about what else you could do with that $400 each month. If you send in $1000 to your mortgage, think about how much else you would be able to do with that money each month if it didn't have to go to the bank. It is likely that you spend $2000 or more on debts each month. What would you be able to do with that $2000 a month, or $24000 a year if you didn't have to send it to someone else? Would you be able to vacation more? Get your dream home? Change jobs to one that pays a little bit less?

Once you start noticing how much you are missing out on because you are trying to pay off your debts, you will start to feel angry. And you can use this anger to motivate you. You will be amazed at how much more quickly you will be able to pay off some of those debts, even the bigger ones, when you have some anger to motivate you to sacrifice, budget, and pay things off.

Getting out of debt is one of those situations where getting some emotions into the process can actually be a good thing. You need to learn how to get mad at your debt, and to feel like you have an attitude of taking no prisoners. You have to decide that to get the debt paid off, you are willing to do anything it takes, even when there is some sacrifice and things are going to get tough for you.

A good way to think about your debt payments and you is that you are a member of the Seal Team 6. You will take out each target of debt one at a time, using a laser-sharp focus and as much precision as possible, until that debt, and the threat is eliminated and you have reached the right objective. Or you can look at it any other way that helps you to visualize getting rid of the debt and staying motivated until it all gets done.

Get Rid of Everything

This one is going to be concerned with a look at credit cards and other debts. It is best to get rid of it all. If you keep any of it around, it is going to cause a lot of issues in your spending. You will see that the credit card or other thing is still there, and it is tempting for you to spend the money, even on things that you don't need.

There are a lot of people who are trying to get out of debt. But they choose to keep the credit card around so that they have something just in case they think that an emergency comes up. But the issue here is that if the credit is available, then it is more likely that you are going to use it. And the thing that you use it on will not be an emergency at all.

The best thing that you can do here is to take all of those credit cards and get rid of them. Go naked when it comes to credit and just use cash for all of the purchases. And if you don't have the cash that you need for that purchase, then you need to wait until you can save up enough.

It may feel a bit strange when you first get rid of all those credit cards. Depending on how many you had and how much you relied on those cards, it is going to feel strange to go to the store and not use them. But dumping them will ensure that when you make payments on the balance, it actually goes down, rather than getting used up again. You may feel vulnerable and exposed. But if you are able to use cash right and budget out your money well, then you will be just fine when you let go of the credit cards.

Think About Using an Accountability Partner

Sometimes you will find that working on your debt journey can feel lonely, especially when you are in a world where everyone seems to be a big consumer and always purchasing something. And since getting out of debt can take a lot longer than it took to get into debt, you may find that having someone who will provide you with moral support through the journey can make it easier. You and your spouse may be able to do it on your own. But finding a mentor or a friend who is willing to step in and provide you with the encouragement that you need can make it much easier.

If you can, find at least one mentor who is already out of debt. This is someone who will have a good understanding of what it takes to get out of debt and see the results that you are looking for, and who can share some of the tips that they used during that time. But anyone, even someone who is working on the process along with you, someone you can support and who will support you in the process as well will make a big difference in the amount of success that you will see.

Blog About Your Progress or Keep a Journal

Keeping track of your progress to financial freedom can make a big difference. This is meant to be an exercise that will keep you focused on the long term results. Even when the debt is gone and you are just working on keeping your money in savings and seeing it grow, this journaling or blogging will make a difference.

When you take some time to write down your victories, struggles, feelings, and anything else that you are dealing with on your debt payoff journey, you will discover that it is going to force you to really think about what is going on with this process. It is going to keep you engaged more in this process than ever before, and will show you just how far you have gone over time. Sometimes, we may feel like we are not getting anywhere because there is still a long way to go to build up the savings or cut down the debt. But when we can look back at the progress that we have made, you will see just how far you have gone.

Plus, there is an added bonus of turning the blog into a way to make an extra amount of money. Some of the best personal finance blogs that are available online right now are the ones who were started by those who detailed the journey that they made out of debt. So, while inspiring others and giving them the help and advice that they need, you can start to make a little bit of money from that blog as well.

Continually Educate Yourself

One of the best things that you are able to do for yourself when it is time to lose the debt and to reach financial freedom - is to spend some time educating yourself about money and how to get out of debt. And with all of the different methods out there to help you get rid of debt and the way the financial world is constantly changing, you will find that there are always things that you can do to help you learn more about debt, financial freedom, investing, and even savings.

You will find that there are a lot of different things that you can do to educate yourself. Read books, listen to podcasts, watch videos, and spend time reading blogs about the subject. Always remember that the more you know about what you want to do with building financial freedom, the more motivated you are going to be to stick with it and see the results. And this knowledge can help you to gain even more control over the situation that is your finances.

Work on Developing your New Habits

When you are ready to get out of debt, it is going to be all about developing some new habits. If you keep up with some of the old habits that you used in the past, then how are you ever going to get out of debt? Those old habits are the ones that you used to get into debt in the first place. Why would you keep using them and hope that all of a sudden, they are going to help you get out of debt?

Obviously, everyone is able to agree that you won't be able to get out of debt by doing the same habits and activities that you did in order to get into debt in the first place. This is why it is so important for you to spend some time developing new habits that will ensure that you can get rid of the debt as quickly as possible.

There are different habits that you are able to use in order to help you develop the new habits that will save you money and cut out debt. You can work with a written budget each month that takes into account the different things that happen. You could start using just cash rather than being tricked into thinking you have more money than you do on a card. You can shop only when you need something. And always search for different ways each day to save money.

The really neat thing here is that changing your habits can really help to change your brain and how it works. And if you are willing to stick with them for even a few months, it can lead to results that will last a lifetime.

Focus on Every Little Step to Get Out of Debt

Removing a mountain of debt may seem like it is really difficult. You may look at your credit card debts, the student loans, the mortgage and more, and feel like you are never going to be able to get out of debt the way that you would like. But the best way to get rid of this mountain of debt is to do it one shovel at a time.

If you just look at the mountain all of the time, it is going to seem like an impossible task. Find a way to just focus on each thing one at a time. Even if you just need to focus on one debt at a time and slowly build it up will make a difference. Focus on the one debt at a time, read motivating articles each day, have a positive thought for the day, say a prayer, and then find something new that you are able to save money on each day. Even listening to a podcast each day can help.

It doesn't have to be a crazy amount of effort to get the results that you want all of the time. a small effort that is done each day can help you keep yourself engaged in the process and will ensure that you are able to keep yourself motivated in the journey to come. It may get hard on occasion, but it is going to ensure that you do get out of debt.

While it may be a little bit of a challenge in order to pay off your debt and take control over your finances, it is so worth it. Developing the right discipline that you need and sticking with all of the plans ahead in order to get out of debt can be so worth it. Some people are going to find that this process is more difficult to stick with than others, but everyone is going to find that it isn't always easy.

But when you take some time to be relentless about overcoming the obstacles during the journey, it makes getting out of debt and building up your own wealth much easier in the long run. Getting out of debt and building wealth is going to be much easier as you get used to it and the longer you stick with it.

PART 2: RENTAL PROPERTIES: AN ULTIMATE SOURCE OF PASSIVE INCOME

CHAPTER 8: WHY SHOULD I CHOOSE RENTAL PROPERTIES AS MY SOURCE OF PASSIVE INCOME?

Everyone has the dream of being able to make money while not having to put in as much work, while they sit back and relax at home, doing the things that they love and that is the most important to them. They are tired of working for their boss and having to make a lot of money for the boss, and never being able to earn what they are worth. The idea of a passive income can seem so appealing, especially when you are trying to work with your own financial freedom, and rental properties can be the best passive income source to help you.

Now, we have talked about some forms of passive income that you can work with when you want to gain your own financial freedom. Passive incomes are basically when you are able to invest your money into a project and over time, you will be able to earn an income without having to do much, if any, work at all. With real estate, you are going to need to put in some work in the beginning. You have to spend time looking at the market, looking for properties, purchasing the property, fixing it up, finding tenants, and maintaining the property. And if you want to turn this into passive income, you will need to go through and do this process a few times.

Over time though, after you have at least a few properties under your name, if not more, you can turn these into a passive income. You can choose a good property management firm to handle your properties for you. They will find tenants, fix up the property, look at any problems that are going on with the property and more, while you get to sit back and collect the rent each month. So, while this is going to require you to put in some work in the beginning, over time you will be able to get a ton of properties and make a big income while letting someone else do the work for you.

Of course, this may sound like something that is just too good to be true. Who could really put in a bit of work for a few years and then walk away without having to worry about doing much while still making an income? But it is a possibility with real estate. This isn't something that will make you rich quick. It is going to take a lot of time and effort on your part, especially in the beginning. But over time, you will find that it is easier for you to grow your empire and make a lot of good money.

Why are rental properties so good for passive income?

There are actually quite a few reasons why working with rental properties can turn into a great passive income investment for your needs, some of the best reasons for this include:

1. Rental income

One of the best things that you are going to notice about rental properties and turning them into a passive income stream is that they are able to provide you with a really stable income stream. What is better than having someone, your tenant, sent to you each month? You have to make sure that you are treating the tenants well and taking care of the property, and you pick out a good property, then you will get a steady stream of income as long as the tenant is able to stay there.

Now, there are going to be two options of real estate properties that are on the market for you to work with. There are going to be the properties that are positively geared and those that are negatively geared. The first one is going to be the kind of property that helps you to produce positive cash flow from the rental income that you collect, and then the second one will not. Your goal to turn this into a passive income source is to choose the ones that are positively geared, especially as a new investor. After all, what is the point of investing your money into a property that will cost more money than you will make?

Do help you are able to get properties that are positive cash flows, you need to make sure that you use a lot of calculators and really do your research ahead of time. This will help you to know how much rent you will be able to charge for the property, how much you should pay for the property to make a profit, and how much it will cost to fix up the building. If all of the numbers result in you making a good amount of money, then it is a good investment.

You won't have to be too involved after you start.

When it comes to how much involvement you are going to need to have when it comes to rental properties, this is one of the best investments for passive income ever. As an investor in rental properties, you can probably guess that there are going to be a lot of tasks to handle. But if you are able to hire a property management firm or just an individual property manager, you will be able to have them take care of all these things for you.

Property management is something that you should consider investing in once you have a few properties under your control. They will take care of the tenants and finding new ones when your property is vacant. They will take care of the daily tasks of the property. They will deal with the tenants, they will collect rent on time, they will fix up the property, and so much more.

There are going to be some fees associated with working with a property management firm. They will usually take about ten percent of the total rental income that you earn unless you have a large apartment where they would make more but be in a smaller area. For single family homes where you make $1000 each month on one property, they would probably earn $100 on each property. But if you have an apartment complex that the manager is helping with, they may take five or six percent instead.

Even though you will need to pay some fees to the property manager, this is the best way for you to turn the rental property into a passive income. They will take over all of the work for you. You will still collect the profits from your rent, after paying the mortgage and the amount to the property manager, but you won't have to be at the property daily. You won't have to focus much on the properties unless you want to be involved. Think about how much freedom of time that this can give you for other endeavors, or the amount that you can make from this.

2. Invest part-time

One thing that you will notice is that with rental properties, you do have the ability to invest yourself only part-time. This means that you will still be able to focus on your regular job, while still making money with your investment into the property. To do this though, you may find that you either need to start out really small and discuss the work schedule with your tenants or work with the property manager to help you out to make this work.

When it comes to this though, you will find that investing in rental properties are going to help you earn a side income, or a second income, without a lot of effort. Keep in mind though that you are able to invest at least part-time into this as well. Just because you have a property manager helping out, especially in the beginning, you still need to invest some of your time into these properties. Always ensure that you are up to date with what is going on with the properties and your business as much as possible.

3. You can invest out of state

Another option that you will get to explore when it comes to using rental properties as a passive income investment is that it opens up the door to investing out of state. You won't have to just limit yourself to investing in the properties that are right in your state or in your town. You are able to explore any other area that you would like.

For example, if you live in the Midwest, you may want to consider purchasing some properties in Florida or somewhere else that is warm. You will definitely need to hire someone else to help out with some of this since you are so far away, but it can open up a lot more doors and opportunities to help you make more money in the process.

If you do decide to invest out of state, take the time to look for the best locations in other states and ensure that you purchase the right property. There are a lot of profitable locations throughout the country and the world, and you need to choose the strategy that you want to use to make it happen.

Take your time to research, and get down to actually see the area and the property before you actually purchase it.

There may be a lot of different options for you to choose when it comes to passive income. But none of them are going to provide you with the amount of profit potential, the amount of flexibility, and the ease for showing you how to make money without having to do all of the work that you do with your regular job! Think about all of the extra freedom of finances and freedom of time that you will gain by doing rental properties.

CHAPTER 9: BASIC STEPS TO PURCHASING A RENTAL PROPERTY

At this point, it is time for you to start out on your rental property. You may find the process of getting started with your own rental property is going to be difficult. If you have never even purchased your own home, then this is going to be even scarier to get started with. The good news is that if you are willing to take your time and research the market, look over the property and do the right inspections, and not rush into the process too quickly, you are going to do fantastic with your investment. Below are the steps that you can do in order to start purchasing your rental property includes:

1. Researching the market

Before you jump into all of this, you need to take some time to research the market. This helps you to learn more about where the best properties are, what you are able to charge for the rent depending on the property and were it is, what you can expect for the prices and if they are likely to go up in the near future, and even some of the laws and the regulations that you need to be aware of when you are becoming a landlord in that area.

The first thing to look at is the market. When it comes to being a rental property investor, a lower economy can actually be a good thing. It means that there are more people who are looking to sell their properties, and they will often sell a really nice property for less than it is worth, or at least less than they would in a better economy. This means that you can get a good deal on the property.

You want to time this out just right though. If you get in right at the bottom of the lower economy, you are in luck. You will be able to purchase the property for a good price. And then, by the time you get it fixed up and ready, the economy or the market will be going back up. You will be able to find more renters and be able to charge a higher rental amount, because of this.

Even if the market seems to be doing the same for a longer period of time, then you can still do well. You just need to take a bit more time to go through and find the properties that you would like to work with. But if you have some patience with it, you will be able to find some good deals in the process.

2. Considering a real estate agent

One thing that you may want to consider when you are working with your first few rental properties is finding a good agent. They know how to run the process, they will be there to advocate on your behalf to get things done, they can do all of the legal paperwork that you need to be done, and they can answer all of your questions. They can be one of the best resources that you can have in order to get started on this endeavor.

The best thing is that the seller is going to be the one who pays for the real estate agent. So you will be able to get this advice and help without having to pay for it at all. If you decide to sell your rental property at a later date and work with an agent, then you will have to pay for them. It is always the seller who is responsible for this.

Since you may not have a lot of experience when it comes to the rental business or to real estate, having an agent can make a big difference. The paperwork on its own can make the big difference that you are looking for as well. You will be able to use their templates and their advice on the purchase price, the contingencies, and more to ensure that everything gets done right at the right time.

3. Finding the first property

Now it is time to start looking for the property that you want to work with. When you are doing this, there are a lot of places that you should consider. And you may find that your real estate agent and a lot of networking can push you in the right direction.

First, take a look in the newspapers, online at real estate places, talk to your real estate agent to see which properties are listed on the MLS, and do a quick walk around town. Just doing these things should provide you with a good idea of which properties are currently being listed in your area, and you can use this information to help you at least find a place to start.

Often, to find the best deals though, you are going to have to get busy and network. Many times the properties that are listed online and in the newspaper are part of the MLS and have an agent working with them. This means the cost may be a bit higher. And usually, they want to be able to make a profit in the process.

When you take some time to network and learn more about the properties in your area, you are more likely to find some good deals. You may hear from a friend that their grandma is looking to sell their home and will do it for a good price if they can move quickly. You may find that the old dilapidated building is being sold at auction in a few weeks and you will be able to make a good profit if you can get it for a good price and do the work. The best deals that you are going to get to help you start with rental properties will be from networking and others who lead you to these deals.

When you are looking at the properties you would like to possibly consider, you also need to consider which amenities are important, how many bedrooms and bathrooms, the location, how close they are to certain attractions and more. Sometimes considering the type of tenant you want to work with can help. If you want to work with families with young children, then properties near parks and schools are important. If you are working with young professionals, then something close to town is the best option. And if you are working with the elderly, then finding a place that is nice and quiet with easy access to clinics and other things they value will work the best.

4. Doing the calculations to see if it is worth the investment

After you are able to find a good property, it is time to do a bit of math and put in some research. There are a ton of properties that can be listed in an area at one time. But not all of these are going to work that well when it comes to being rental properties. If you end up spending too much on the mortgage of the property, or the combination of the mortgage and on all of the fixes that you need to do on the property, then you won't be able to charge a rental price that is high enough.

The first thing to consider is how much you are hoping to get the property for, or how much it is being listed at the time. You can then do a few calculations, either with some research online or with the help of a mortgage lender, to figure out how much your taxes, insurance, and mortgage payment on that property are going to be each month.

Once you have that number, it is time to figure out how much it is going to cost you in order to fix up the property. You should take some time to do a walk through to see the property and determine if it is going to need a lot of work. You can then talk to some of the contractors in your area, and look up prices to see how much you think the property is going to take to fix up. Write this number down, and add another 20 to 30 percent to it. There are always additional things that come up that need to be fixed and taken care of. If these things don't come up, you get to pocket the extra. But if they do come up, at least you were prepared to handle them.

Take the number that you came up with for repairs and divide it up by how long you get to pay it if you took out a loan to handle those repairs. Then add this monthly payment to the amount that you will owe with the mortgage. From this number, you will want to add in the amount of profit that you would like to earn each month. Be reasonable here. There are very few places around where you can make a couple thousand a month in profit on the rent for each month, especially since you still have to pay for the mortgage and all the repair costs. Adding in a few hundred on each property is usually a good bet.

Once you have this number, it is time to move on and take a look at the rents that are allowed in that area. You should try to look up properties that are being rented out or have been offered for rent within the last six months, that are similar to yours. Look for ones in the same area of town, that have the same number of bedrooms and bathrooms, the same square footage and so on. Once you find the properties that are similar, take some time to figure out how much, on average, these are able to charge tenants for rent.

When you look at that number, does that match up with the number that you got before? Will you be able to make the mortgage, repair costs, and the profits that you want? If it meets that, or the rental prices are even higher than what you came up with, then this is a good deal. You should definitely consider making an offer on it and using this as one of your properties.

If the numbers don't add up, and your number is higher than the average rent, then there are a few things to consider. First, do you think that you can get the property for a significantly lowered price? How low do you think the price will go? Are there any of your projected repairs that you can get rid of without harming the overall price of the property and save money? Are you willing to take a little bit less profit on the property to get the number done?

If you are cutting back on a few places and still don't think that you will be able to make a profit then it is time to look at another property. This one may make a nice family home or a property for someone else. But it isn't going to provide you with the things that you need to be a good rental property.

5. Putting in an offer

After you have had some time to look at the property, do your calculations, and compare to some of the other options on the market, it is time to put in an offer with the seller. You should have a good idea about the maximum that you are willing to spend. This number should be the highest amount that you can afford on the property and still make a profit with the rent each month.

Write that number down and keep it close. But when it comes to sending in a purchase agreement and the price that you offer at first, you should go with a number that is lower than this. It is likely that the seller will want to negotiate with you a little bit. If you come in at the highest price you will pay, then you will have no room to negotiate with them at all.

Start out with a smaller number, but have the idea that they will probably want to do a bit of back and forth with you. If the seller does come back and agree to that smaller offer, then you scored a big deal. You were able to get the property for less than what you had budgeted for, and that means you get to keep more of the income in the process.

But since your seller is most likely going to want to negotiate and try to get the price higher, at least this gives you some wiggle room to keep it near the number that you want. Don't let the negotiations go on for so long though that you end up agreeing to a price that is higher than you can afford. It is easy to let your emotions get the best of you and to stick with a property because you have spent a lot of time and energy on it so far. But it is best for you to use logic and get out when the numbers get too high.

Hopefully, you and the seller are able to come up with a price that works the best for both of you. If so, you will both sign the purchase agreement and then all of the other work comes in. If you find that the seller and you are not able to come to a good agreement about what you would like the price to be, it is fine to walk away. You can then take this time and energy in order to search for another property that will meet your needs and your price point a bit better.

6. Doing the inspections

No matter what condition the property looks to be in before you purchase it, make sure that you are taking the time to go through and do your inspections. This is something that a lot of beginners in the world of real estate will forget about. They think that the inspection isn't necessary. To them, the property looks perfect, the seller is a nice person so they wouldn't lie, and that the inspection is going to cost too much money for the time.

But since you are most likely an investor and not someone who is an expert in the field of real estate, forgoing the inspection can be a really bad idea. You never know what big things may be hiding in the property, and it is always best to know about them ahead of time, rather than assuming they aren't there and then being surprised later on when you are the one who has to deal with them.

If the inspector comes in and finds that there is a major thing that needs to be fixed, you get the upper hand. Your purchase agreement should include a contingency about the home inspection. You can then take the information from the inspector and ask the seller to reduce the price of the property so that you can make the fixes, ask them to fix it for you, or you can walk away if the seller is unable or unwilling to help out with any of this.

Remember, if you find out about one of the problems after you close on the property, you are stuck. And you definitely don't want to have a $5000 expense on top of your purchase price and expenses just because of something that could have been found in the home inspection, or something that you could have made the seller deal with instead.

7. Checking out the title

Another thing that you can consider working on here is checking out the title on the property. This helps you to know who may have a claim on the property if there are any liens or anything else that you need to worry about. If the seller doesn't take the time to fix these before you close on the property, it could cause some issues for you.

Going through and purchasing title insurance and doing the title check can protect you. This will allow you to check what the seller needs to fix on the title before you will purchase it. Just because there is a lien on the property doesn't mean that it is something to be worried about. For example, if the seller stills owe a mortgage on the home, the mortgage company will have a lien on the title to ensure they get paid. The seller will pay the mortgage company with the money you pay them, so that won't be an issue.

But if there are any other claims or liens on the title, then these are things that need to be taken care of as quickly as possible. This will ensure that you are able to take the title clear and clean, and you won't have to worry about someone coming after you later for taxes, a missed bill that isn't yours, or a family member of the previous seller who tries to claim the property as their own.

8. Closing on the property

If you are working with a real estate agent, they will be able to walk you through the process of closing on the property. But often a real estate lawyer or attorney will be able to do most of the work to provide you with the information that you need in order to get the property closed.

Before you sign the papers, make sure to take some time in order to go through the property and double check that it all looks good. A walkthrough right before signing can help you see whether the seller actually fixed up the things that they were supposed to, and can help you to ensure that the seller, or someone else, didn't come through and mess up or destroy everything. Remember, once you sign the papers, the property is yours and you have no legal recourse if something wasn't done right.

Once you and the seller sign the papers, and the money is transferred over to the seller (your mortgage company will usually write out a check to the seller to do this), then the property is yours! Congratulations on owning your first rental property and on getting started with seeing some big results in the process with your investment.

9. Fixing it up quickly

Once you own the property, it is time to get to work fixing it up as quickly as possible. Remember that the longer the property is left empty, the more you have to pay out of pocket for the mortgage and interest, insurance, taxes, and more. If you can keep this down to a few months or less, then you will be able to get someone else into the property and paying for those amounts.

Before you signed on the property, you should have gained a great idea of what you have to pay for and get fixed inside the property. But once those papers are signed, get inside and get them done. Line up the contractors ahead of time so they can get in the day of, or within a few days of, closing to get their work done. If there are things that you plan to work on yourself, then get into the property and start working on those as soon as you can.

Messing around on this step is going to cost you. It will lead you to hold onto the property for longer than necessary without making any money or profit in the process and wasting a lot of money instead. The sooner that you can get the tenants inside and paying rent, the happier you will be in terms of making a profit on this.

10.Finding the right tenants

Another thing that you need to consider when you are getting into rental properties is to find the right tenants. The right tenant can make being a landlord a breeze. They will take good care of the property. They will follow the rules of the lease. They won't call you for each and everything that comes up or bothers them. They will stay for the full term of their lease, and maybe even stay for two or three or more years so you have a steady stream of income without having to spend time and money finding new tenants. In short, they can make being a landlord and earning this passive income seem like a breeze.

But a bad tenant can make things really difficult and can make you want to pull out your hair and run away from being a landlord at all. A bad tenant can destroy your property and leave you to try to fix it. They will call you at all hours of the day or night to complain and say that there are emergencies that aren't there. They will miss out on a lot of the rental payments that are due to you, and will just cause a lot of problems.

Many of these bad tenants will hopefully be gone soon. Even though this means that you have to go through and find another tenant, at least they are gone and out of your hair. But sometimes the bad tenants can be so bad that you will have to try to evict them. No matter where you live, this can be a really long and tedious process that costs you a ton of money just to get your property back.

This is why it is so important to properly screen the tenants you are going to invite into your property. You should consider doing a background check to see if they can afford the place and if they have any criminal record. Consider whether they have broken leases in the past if they have a steady income source without job hoping over the years and so on.

In addition, make sure that your tenant is willing to sign a lease. This is there to protect you and the tenant so it is important. Inside, you should have information on the lease, the parties involved, and a list of the things that you are responsible for as the landlord and what the tenant is responsible for. This is a document both parties can refer back to if there are any questions that come up. If your tenant isn't willing to sign the lease, this means that something is wrong, and you should skip to the next applicant in line.

11.Maintaining the property

After the tenants move in, it is going to be your job to take care of the property, to handle any concerns that come up, and to be there if an emergency in the property happens, such as the heat going out. The exact things that you will be responsible for on the property will vary based on the area you are in, and the terms of your lease.

For the first property or two, you may decide to do the work on your own. It is possible to hire a property manager, but you may not bring enough in for rent to make this work so you will have to handle it on your own. You can find some low-cost repairmen and others who are willing to help you out when things get above your own personal knowledge base. After you have a few properties under your belt and make enough out of the properties, it will make more sense to hire a property manager who can handle the work for you.

Finding a good property to use for a rental property is something that can take some time and can be a bit challenging in some cases. Many times we are so excited to start making this new stream of income, and the thought of turning it into a passive income can make us impatient. But the truth is, this process could take a few months or more depending on how long it takes to find a property, how long it takes to close on the property, and how long it takes to find tenants and getting it started.

This can be frustrating, but you don't want to rush into a deal that you aren't ready for. You want to take your time, know when the property is actually a good one, do your due diligence to make sure that the property is passing inspections and will be good for the tenant, and find the right tenants to place inside. Once you are able to do this, you will be amazed at how much easier it is for you to make a profit on this property, and any of the other properties you choose to work with.

CHAPTER 10: HOW TO TURN YOUR PROPERTY INTO A PASSIVE INCOME

Now to the big event! We have been taking some time in this guidebook to talk about financial freedom and some of the great benefits of gaining your own freedom with your money, no matter what stage of life you are in. There are a lot of Americans who are stuck paying most of their paychecks to a creditor all of the time, and never getting the benefit of being able to use that money the way that they would like. With financial freedom, you will find that it is easier than ever for you to take that money you earn, and put it into any other investments that you want, to build up good savings, or just use it in any way that you would like.

You will find that it is going to take a lot of hard work, and a good amount of investment in your time in order to turn your rental properties into a passive income. It is unlikely that your first or even second property will be enough to make you a ton of income, even though the extra money may be useful to help you pay off debts and gain some financial freedom faster. But you still need to invest money and time into these to even get that.

But over time, with a lot of work, and gathering more and more properties over a few years, you will find that you can really earn a passive income. If you have ten properties where you make $300 in profit on each one, and you could almost replace your full-time income. And as you pay off the mortgages of these properties, using your rent payments, and you keep charging the same amount of rent, the profit on that property could jump u to the full $1000 (or whatever you charge for rent) without any extra work on your part!

One of the best ways that you can earn the financial freedom that you deserve is to work with rental properties. But now that you own a rental property (thanks to the steps that we talked about in the previous chapter), you may be wondering how you are going to be able to turn it into a passive income. Some of the steps that you can take to make this happen include:

1. Do your research

Before you start the process of looking for a property to purchase, one that is going to help you create a passive income, you have to get to work, do some research, and do your homework. You have to understand all the things that you need to do in order to become a landlord and what it entails to rent out your properties to tenants.

Some of the things that you should take the time to research about in your area include the tax implications you will need to deal with, the legal rights and responsibilities that you have as a landlord in your state, and how you will plan to manage that property each day. You also need to understand how you are going to deal with problems that come up, as described by a writer for Fox Business when they spent time as a landlord for a bit:

We've spent far too many weekends painting and cleaning our properties between tenants. We've driven to and arranged countless meetings to discuss remodeling projects and repairs. We've had to deal with a whole host of random issues such as late rent payments, feuding neighbors, and secret pets. Once, one of our properties was even left in total shambles - with oil-stained carpet, missing doors, busted windows, and broken everything."

While there are things that you can do to try and avoid some of these issues when you bring tenants into your property, it is important to realize that these things do happen, and they may be some of the things that you have to deal with when you are working as a landlord and renting out. The information above is the reality of using real estate as a passive income, especially if you are not careful with the types of tenants you allow into the building. This isn't to say that everything is bad and that you won't be able to make any income from it. But you do need to make sure that you are aware of the reality, and plan ahead if you really want to turn this into a passive income.

2. Make sure that you find a property with positive cash flow

The number one thing that you want to focus on when it comes to picking out a good rental property is that you need to make sure you find one that has a positive cash flow. This means that when you get a renter in there, they will pay you enough that you will take home some profit. It isn't going to help you to gain the financial freedom that you want from the property if you don't earn a profit on it, or you lose money on it.

This means that even with all the expenses that are associated with owning the property and keeping it look nice, and keeping it in good shape, you are earning a profit rather than losing money or breaking even. You will need to make a considerable amount of profit. And the best way to do this is to start by purchasing the property at a low enough price where you will be able to charge a good amount of rent and make that profit.

Another thing to consider is looking at some market research and see which areas near you have the least amount of tenant turnover, and which ones have the

highest. The more turnover there is with tenants, the harder it will be for you to keep the building filled and for you to earn a consistent profit from the rent that you make.

Once you pick out an area that you think will keep the turnover of tenants down to a minimum, it is time to come up with a careful vetting process before letting any tenants move in. You want to find tenants that are able to actually afford the rent that you are charging and to lessen the chances that you will have to go through the process, and the costs, of evicting them.

And although you may want to take the time and catch a diamond in the rough of fixing up homes that are in disrepair, this is not always the best path to choose to go with when it comes to picking a property that will make a passive income. You can pick out some properties that need a little bit of work if they are really well priced, but going with those that are falling apart and dilapidated may take up too much time and money to help you really make any income from them.

3. Look for a property that doesn't need a lot of management

In addition to taking your time and doing a lot of research to find a property that will provide you with a positive amount of cash flow, you will want to make sure that any rental property you choose doesn't require a lot of hands-on management. You do not want to spend all of your time managing your property. You may already have a regular 9 to 5 job to focus on, and you don't want to spend all of your time trying to manage this property either. And if the property takes a lot of hands-on management, any property manager you find is going to charge you more as well, which cuts into your profits.

While it may be tempting to think about looking at condos or vacation homes, and while these may seem exciting and a great option, these are going to cause some problems when you are ready to manage them. Vacation homes, in particular, are going to take a lot of management. Since there are new renters coming in every weekend or week in most cases, you are going to be responsible for taking care of the property and making sure it is set and ready to go for the next tenants. This is even more difficult if you don't' live in the same state as the property.

Either you can spend this time working on doing all the maintenance and clean up each week, in the example of the vacation home, or you will have to pay a lot more money for a property management company or cleaners to come and do this for you. It can also be a lot of work to keep renters on the property all the year when most will only be there for a few days, maybe a few weeks at a time. This makes it harder to get a steady income on the property throughout the year.

4. Hire a management company to help, and outsource as much work as possible.

If you own ten properties and have to do all of the work of finding tenants, repairing things in the property, collecting rent, dealing with issues on the property, and everything else that comes with being a landlord, then these rental properties are not really going to be a passive income. But if you are able to hire a property management company to help run the properties, and outsource as much work as possible, then this can actually turn into a passive income.

Hiring a management company to help run your properties will be the final step that you need to take in order to turn these rental properties into your passive income stream. These teams are going to be able to take on a lot of the tasks and the other responsibilities that you are already handling as a landlord. They can also handle all of the other issues and problems that come up during the daily dealings of the property so that you don't have to.

Depending on the profit that your rental properties are bringing in from one month to the next, you may want to consider if there are other types of work that you are able to outsource in the property. They can help to do with painting, repairing things, mowing and more. If you are not sure who you use, you can talk to your property management team. They often have references for cheap and reliable labor who can help with these things.

You don't want to completely run out of the picture when you hire a property manager. This is your source of income, and you are responsible for how the property management company behaves to your tenants and more. It is smart to spend some time checking in on the properties and on the daily activities of them from time to time. But hiring one of these management companies means that you can concentrate on other endeavors, go traveling, and do other things without focusing all of your energy on your properties all of the time.

While there is a good deal of risk and investment of time and money when you get started on a rental property, it is one of the best ways that you are able to work on creating a good source of passive income. And there is nothing better for helping you to work on gaining your financial freedom and retiring early!

CONCLUSION

Thank for making it through to the end of ***Retire Early with Real Estate***, let's hope it was informative and able to provide you with all of the tools you need to achieve your goals whatever they may be.

The next step is to get your finances in order. If you have a lot of debts and a lot of trouble managing your money from one month to the next, then you may find it almost impossible to either get the mortgage you want or to save up enough money to purchase the property with cash. When you take some of our tips in this guidebook to set up your own budget and to start a good emergency fund, it becomes so much easier to see the results that you want, without feeling stressed out.

Once you have a budget in place and can get some of your debts paid down, while also working to start up an emergency fund and fix up your credit score, it is time to work with getting your rental property. While there are a lot of other options you can choose to work with in terms of coming up with a passive income stream, none are as profitable or as effective as working with rental properties. We spent some time inside talking about some of the steps you can take to purchase your first rental property and look at the benefits of going with this option over some of the others.

When you are ready to retire early and actually enjoy the life that you have to live, then rental properties and other real estate endeavors can be the right option for you. This guidebook is the perfect tool to help you reach those goals and see the results that you want.

Finally, if you found this book useful in any way, a review on Amazon is always appreciated!

www.ingramcontent.com/pod-product-compliance
Lightning Source LLC
LaVergne TN
LVHW022318200926
848481LV00004B/1372